Why do I have to?

by the same author

Asperger Syndrome in Young Children
A Developmental Approach for Parents and Professionals
Laurie Leventhal-Belfer and Cassandra Coe
ISBN 978 1 84310 748 4

of related interest

My Social Stories Book
Edited by Carol Gray and Abbie Leigh White
Illustrated by Sean McAndrew
ISBN 978 1 85302 950 9

Personal Hygiene? What's that Got to Do with Me?
Pat Crissey
Illustrated by Noah Crissey
ISBN 978 1 84310 796 5

Caring for Myself
A Social Skills Storybook
Christy Gast and Jane Krug
Photographs by Kotoe Laackman
ISBN 978 1 84310 872 6 (hardback)
ISBN 978 1 84310 887 0 (paperback)

Joey Goes to the Dentist
Candace Vittorini and Sara Boyer-Quick
ISBN 978 1 84310 854 2

Why do I have to?

A Book for Children Who Find Themselves Frustrated by Everyday Rules

Laurie Leventhal-Belfer

Illustrated by Luisa Montaini-Klovdahl

Jessica Kingsley Publishers
London and Philadelphia

First published in 2008
by Jessica Kingsley Publishers
116 Pentonville Road
London N1 9JB, UK
and
400 Market Street, Suite 400
Philadelphia, PA 19106, USA

www.jkp.com

Library of Congress Cataloging in Publication Data
Leventhal-Belfer, Laurie.
Why do I have to? : a book for children who find themselves frustrated by everyday rules / Laurie Leventhal-Belfer.
 p. cm.
 ISBN 978-1-84310-891-7 (pb : alk. paper) 1. Obedience--Juvenile literature. 2. Frustration--Juvenile literature. 3. School children--Conduct of life--Juvenile literature. I. Title.
 BJ1459.L48 2008
 179'.9--dc22

2007051882

British Library Cataloguing in Publication Data
A CIP catalogue record for this book is available from the British Library

ISBN 978 1 84310 891 7

Printed and bound in the United States by
Thomson-Shore, 7300 Joy Road, Dexter, MI 48130

In memory of my father, Harry Leventhal
A man who had the gift of transforming everyday events into
magical stories

Acknowledgements

This book could not have been developed if it were not for the endless examples provided by the parents who participated in the "Friends Program" concerning the roadblocks that arose between them and their children. These barriers could make daily events, such as getting dressed or going to school, challenging at times, at other times rewarding, and at other times overwhelming. We owe to these families our deepest appreciation for all that they have taught us about their children. Through our long-term relationships with these families we have learned how easily we can be trapped into a never-ending discussion about a child's current interest or reasons why they feel what is being asked of them is not fair. We also want to thank our colleagues who took the time to read over our text and offer helpful advice: Monika Perez, Mary Jo Huetteman, Marci Schwartz, Angela Huerta, Teri Wiss, Rebecca Fineman, Mirella Minnich, and Luisa's boys: Kris, Lars, and Nils. Lastly, I want to thank Howard for his patience, love, critical eye, and for never asking me, "Why do I have to read…?"

Contents

Preface for Children

This book is for you if you get frustrated with adults who expect you to follow certain rules or to do things that you think you should not have to do. Sometimes these rules can make you feel confused and upset. It is hoped that this book will help you understand why such rules exist and how you might be able to make things work better. You may also want to know that other children and some adults find some of these rules to be very annoying as well. What the adults have learned is that if they are going to be able to do the things they want to do they have to follow many different rules at home, at work, and with their friends.

Preface for Adults

This book is for parents and professionals working with children who have difficulty coping with the hassles of everyday life. These children may at times look and act like little adults. They may have no difficulty spending hours alone in their room building a city out of blocks, playing a video game, or telling a grandparent about their favorite baseball team. Yet when their plans are interrupted, they can transform into toddlers having a prize-winning tantrum. At these moments, these children may appear rigid, demanding, quirky, inattentive, self-absorbed, oppositional, or vulnerable, which are behaviors that naturally can make adults question a child's capacity to cope with the demands being placed on him or her. These same children may be very creative in coming up with an endless barrage of questions about the expectations that adults have of them, and very detailed reasons for why these rules are not fair. Often these children are not as interested in the answers as much as they are in winning more time to do a desired activity or support for their position.

As you will see, all of our stories follow a similar pattern. First, they acknowledge how the child is feeling and empathize with him or her, rather than dismiss the child's frustrations or go directly to how he or she should behave. Then the stories provide an explanation for why such a rule exists. Each story ends with a positive statement affirming the benefit of a more adaptive coping style. Each story is supported with concrete suggestions of more adaptive ways of coping with a specific rule along with an invitation for the child to come up with his or her own suggestions.

One of the biggest challenges in working with these children is getting the strategies that may work in one setting to generalize into different settings and situations. This book is designed to provide a springboard for developing empathic stories attuned to children's individual strengths and needs. What is important for you to remember is that children will not be able to automatically read a story, discuss it, and then incor-porate it into their daily lives. Rather, it will take a great deal of work and practice before a child is able to integrate spontane-ously a new coping strategy without external support.

For these reasons, we suggest that you select a specific story that addresses a challenging time for you and your child. Next, we suggest that you read that story with your child for several days, identifying specific coping strategies that might work for him or her. If your child is the very rigid type, who tends to fight change, then we suggest that from the start your plan should include more than one solution and that you practice taking different approaches at different times. For example, on some days your child may look at a book at naptime and other days he or she may listen to music or draw. Lastly, it is suggested that you implement the story, keeping track of the times that your child experiences success as well as those times when roadblocks get in the way. It may be very helpful to keep a weekly chart of the child's progress on a daily basis. It is very easy to forget the times when your strategies are working after a very difficult afternoon!

A behavioral chart is provided at the end of the book (Appendix 2) to help keep track of your child's progress. At the top of the chart, the parent or child writes down the specific positive behavior that the child is trying to achieve, for example, "being the boss of my body – no hitting, kicking, or hurting other people, myself or other objects." The child receives a positive mark for each time that they are able to maintain their goal. At the end of the day, the parent and child review the chart and the parent delivers a small reward the child has earned. For some children a chart is not necessary because a treat in the car ride to school or fewer accidents on the playground is motivation enough. For others, just seeing the number of stars they accumulate is a sufficient incentive, and for still others a concrete reward may be required, such as a chocolate chip for each checkmark or ten minutes on the computer if the child earns a certain number of checks. The chart also provides helpful information about the days and times when your child experiences both success and difficulty, which is information that may be used to fine-tune the child's story, strategies, and rewards. If the issue you are working on arises primarily at school, then it will be important to work in collaboration with your child's teacher in the design and application of a chart that represents the different components of the child's school day. The child can then bring the chart home after school for the same type of reward system. Lastly, remember that this process is hard for both you and your child. For these reasons, it is recommended that you work on only one issue at a time and make certain you celebrate the successes that both you and your child work hard to achieve.

1

Rules that may be Frustrating at Home

I hate it when everyone tells me that I have to hurry up or I
will be late for school!

Why do I have to go to school on time?

It can be very frustrating when adults tell you to "turn off the
TV" in the middle of a show, or "stop spacing out" and get ready
for school. You may not feel that you are "spacing out" when
you are looking at an interesting book, watching a video, or
building something special with your Lego. What your parents
are saying is that you need to get ready to go to school so that
you will be there on time.

Every school has a set time when the children need to arrive
so that they have enough time to be with their friends and learn
all of the things that their teacher has to teach them. If you are
late for school you may not have time to play with a friend, do a
favorite activity, or talk with your teacher. Your mom and dad

may also be late for work. School is a place to learn new things and make new friends.

It might help if I:

- record my favorite show to watch after school

- pick out my clothes and food for breakfast the night before; make a picture chart to remind me what I need to do

- take a snack to have in the car or at school during recess in case I am still hungry.

Do you have any ideas that might help make going to school easier for you?

Ready for school.

I do not like wearing shoes and a coat when I go
outside.

Why do I have to wear shoes and a jacket when I go outside?

You may not like the feeling of socks and shoes on the bottom
of your feet. The problem with being barefoot outside is that
you could hurt yourself if you stepped on something and cut
your foot.

You may also not like to wear a jacket when you go outside.
The problem with this is that if you do not wear a coat when it is
cold or wet outside you may catch a cold and have to stay inside
and take "icky"-tasting medicine.

It's fun to be able to play outside all year round.

It might help if I:

- ✏ rub my feet before trying to put on socks, so that the socks don't feel so "icky"

- ✏ ask my parents if they can find different socks that feel better on my feet[*]

- ✏ wear my coat over a soft shirt so that I do not have to feel the jacket on my arms

- ✏ pick out a pair of shoes that are "cool" looking and comfortable; it will also help if I can put the shoes on and take them off all by myself.

Do you have other ideas to make wearing a coat or shoes easier for you?

Ready to go.

---

[*] Parents can look at websites such as www.TicTacToe.net or www.SensoryComfort.com for ideas.

I do not understand why everybody has to eat at the same time.

Why do I have to sit at the table to eat when I am not hungry?

It would be nice if you only had to eat when you feel like it. The problem with this is that your body may need food even when you don't feel hungry. Some people do not notice that they are hungry when they are busy doing things that they like, such as playing outside. Some people only like food that looks, feels, smells, or tastes a certain way. When your body does not have enough food, you may feel tired and grumpy. You may forget that your parents cannot make you anything you want whenever you are hungry. Parents need time to work, eat, and rest.

Everybody's body needs nutrition every day so that they can stay strong and healthy.

It might help if I:

- if it is hard to sit still, try a different chair, a wiggle cushion, or putting a box on the floor so my feet have a place to rest

- talk with my parents about what bugs me the most about mealtime and ways to make it work better, like having different foods or saving part of the meal to eat later if I get hungry

- think of things that might be fun to talk about at the table, such as the best, worst, or silliest things that happened during the day.

Do you have any ideas that might make mealtime work better for you?

Ready for dinner.

I don't understand why adults tell me I need to take a nap or go to sleep when I'm not tired!

Why do I have to rest when I am not tired?

It is easy to understand why you think you should only have to rest or sleep when you feel very tired. The trick is that your body may need to rest even when you do not feel tired. You might be surprised to know that adults, just like kids, need time to rest and do quiet things. Both children and adults need to sleep to stay healthy and strong.

During rest time I could:

- quietly look at books

- listen to a story on tape

- quietly draw in a drawing book

- talk quietly with a favorite stuffed animal.

Do you have any ideas that might make rest times work better for you?

Ready for resting.

I don't understand why grown-ups keep bugging me about going to the bathroom when I don't have to go!

Why do I have to go to the bathroom when I don't need to?

There are some times and places where it is very hard to get to the bathroom right away so it is very important to try to go to the bathroom ahead of time. Some of these places are when traveling by car or plane, or going on a bike ride. Other places where it can be hard getting to the bathroom on time are at the movies, in a store, during a class, or at a park.

You might think that you should only have to go to the bathroom when you can feel that you have to go. Sometimes, if you wait until you feel like you have to go, you might have an accident. It can be hard to tell if you need to go to the bathroom when you are busy playing a game or watching a show. At those times, you may be paying more attention to the show than to how your body feels.

It feels good when you are able to go to the bathroom on time, before you have an accident.

I might try:

- going to the bathroom before starting a new activity
- before saying, "no," counting to five and really listening to my body to see if it might be sending me a very quiet message
- taking a favorite book or magazine to look at while I sit on the toilet.

Do you have any ideas that might help you go to the bathroom on time?

Ready for play.

I don't think it's fair that I have to share all of my toys with other kids!

Why do I have to share toys if I am still using them?

Sometimes you may not want to let someone else play with your toys because you are afraid that they might break a toy or change the way that you had the toys arranged. When you play with your brothers and sisters or a friend, you need to share your toys with them. Sharing a toy does not mean that you will lose the toy or not have another chance to play with it. Nobody likes to play with someone who will not share their toys. It can be hard to share, but it is fun to play with other kids.

It might help if I:

- go through the toys with Mom or Dad and see if there is a "special" toy that I would have a hard time sharing, and put it away when I will be with siblings or friends

- remember that when someone is playing with a toy that I want, I cannot ask them to give me the toy right away; I also cannot grab the toy from them, if I cannot think of something else to do, I can ask an adult for help

- ask a parent to use a timer so everyone will have a chance to play with a specific toy.

Do you have any ideas that might make sharing your toys easier for you?

Ready to share.

I get mad when grown-ups tell me that I have to get off the computer or stop watching TV before my game or show is finished!

Why do I have to turn off the computer or the TV before my game or show is over?

It may seem unfair to you that adults expect you to stop playing a computer or video game before you are finished playing the game, or turn off the TV before a show is over. The reason you cannot play the computer or watch TV for as long as you want is that there are other things that you need to do. Some of the other things you might need to do are go to a class, finish your homework, have dinner, take a bath, or go to bed!

If you stayed on the computer or watched a video for as long as you wanted, then you might not have time to do the other things that you need to do. Playing on the computer or watching a show can be fun when you are able to stop without getting upset.

It might help if I:

- know ahead of time how long I can play on the computer or watch TV each day and have the time on a chart that I can check before I begin; set a timer so that I have a five-minute warning before my time is up; agree that if I go over time, I will lose those minutes the next time I play

- only play games that can stop at any time without losing points, or get a memory chip for the game system that will save my place; I may also only want to watch shows that I have recorded so I can finish watching the show at a different time

- find other activities that I might enjoy doing like artwork, board games, playing Frisbee or Lego.

Do you have any ideas that might help make stopping the computer, video game, or television easier for you?

Ready to do something else!

I don't understand why I get in trouble for talking about things that I think are interesting!

Why do I have to stop talking about things that I like?

It can be frustrating to get into trouble for talking about things that you really like. It is important to remember that not everyone likes the same things that you do and nobody likes to hear someone talking about the same thing for a long time. For example, your friends may not want to hear everything you know about a baseball team, trains, or computers. It is not that your ideas are bad. It is just that other people may not find them as interesting as you do. It can be hard to listen to another person talk when they do not give you a chance to speak. It is fun to share your ideas with your teacher and classmates and to learn new ideas from them as well.

It might help if I:

-  try to make sure that I only say two things at a time and hold the rest of my ideas in an imaginary (pretend) folder or write them down!

- remind myself I will get another chance to say more after other people have a turn at talking

- make a record book about my favorite subjects so that I do not have to worry about forgetting important information.

Do you have any ideas that might help you remember not to do all the talking and make sure to listen to what others have to say?

> What do you want to do?

Ready to listen as well as talk.

2

Rules that may be Frustrating about Friends

I don't like it when I have to be with my friend for the entire play date!

Why do I have to play with my friend all of the time?

It can be frustrating when a parent expects you to spend all of the time with your friend during a play date. Sometimes you just want to be alone, play with an imaginary friend, or work on an activity that you were doing before your friend came over.

It helps to remember that you would not like it if a friend ignored you when you went over to their house to play. When a friend comes over, they are expecting to spend all of their time playing with you, not with your mother, your siblings, by themselves, or just watching you do an activity. It is fun to have a friend over to hang out and to play.

I could:

- write up a plan with my parent about what I might do with a friend during our play date; the list might include letting my friend pick an activity to do in my room, having a snack, and playing in the backyard; I might have my mom call my friend's mom so that my friend knows the plan ahead of time; it can also help if my mom writes down the plan so that we can both see it

- ask an adult for some ideas of what we might do if we cannot come up with something that we would like to play together

- remember that I can play by myself after my friend goes home.

Do you have any ideas of what might help you stay with a friend during a play date?

Ready to share play dates.

I hate it when I have to pretend to like a present when I think it is ugly or for babies!

Why do I have to say "thank you" for a present that I do not like?

You might feel annoyed that you have to say "thank you" for something you do not like. Telling a friend that you do not like the present that they gave you may hurt their feelings. It is not nice or funny to hurt another person's feelings. Saying "thank you" does not mean that you like the gift. It just means that it was nice that they thought of bringing you a present.

It's fun to have friends come over to visit or as guests for a party.

I should try to remember that:

- as soon as I receive a gift, I should say "thank you" even if I don't like it

- on another day, I might be able to exchange the gift for something I like better

- after the party or visit, I could give the gift to someone who might enjoy it more than I do

- I have other toys that I can play with at home.

Do you have any ideas of what would help you say something nice to a person who just gave you a gift that you do not like?

Ready to be nice about presents.

I wish I didn't have to leave the house when I feel like staying home!

Why do I have to go to a friend's house when I would rather stay home?

It can be very hard to leave your house to go visit a friend when you are in the middle of doing something you enjoy at home. You might have been frustrated when you had a play date set up, but your friend couldn't make it. It might help to remember the times that you had fun playing with other kids at their houses or at the park. When you go to visit a friend, you may get to play with different toys than you have at home or do activities that need more than one person.

It's fun to go over to a friend's house to play.

I can:

- remember that I can continue working on my activity when I return from my play date

- take a toy to my friend's house that I would feel comfortable sharing with my friend

- think of some things that we might like to play together, such as tag, board games, or Lego.

Do you have any ideas of what might help you leave the house and go to visit a friend when you do not feel like leaving your house?

Ready to go out visiting.

Nobody plays the game the right way!

Why do I have to let other kids play a game the "wrong" way?

You may like to play a game by the rules that you are used to or that you have made up. What you may not know is that other people may have learned to play the same game a different way. Just because their rules are different from your rules, it does not mean that they are wrong. People often learn how to play the same game in different ways. It is important to remember that nobody likes to be told that they are playing the game "wrong" or "cheating," just because they play a game a different way. If you are playing a make-believe game, a good rule to follow is that whoever begins the game gets to make up the rules. Your teacher may also be able to help the class choose a set of rules for playground games, and then write them down so that everyone can see them.

It is fun to play with different kids, even if they play the same game different ways.

It may help if I:

- take turns playing the same game different ways

- ask an adult to clarify for everyone what the rules are

- rather than argue over the rules and ruin the recess, let my friend choose another game or activity for us to play.

Do you have any ideas of what might help you play a game a different way than you are used to?

Ready to play a different way.

I don't think it's fair that I have to say "I'm sorry," when other people do something to me first!

Why do I have to apologize to other kids for hurting them if they hurt me first?

It may not seem fair that you have to apologize for hurting another child if they said something mean to you first. If someone hurts your feelings by saying something mean or doing something like taking a toy that you were playing with, then you can tell them "Stop bothering me!" If a person hurts you by pushing, grabbing, or hitting then you should tell the other person to "Stop hurting me!" If the other person does not stop bothering or hurting you, then you should go to an adult, such as a teacher or parent, and ask for help.

However, if you hit, push, kick, or grab the other person back, then both of you are wrong. *It is never OK to hurt another person.*

Your home, school, and neighborhood are places where you should always feel safe.

It may help if I:

- tell the other child to stop bothering me and then go find something else to do

- take five deep breaths and try not to get into an argument with the other person

- go ask an adult for help; I have to remember that the adult may not say anything to the other child right away, as long as I am safe; when the adult is not watching the other children, they can help me think about what to do if this happens to me again.

Do you have any ideas of what might help you stay calm when another person upsets you?

Ready to stop fighting.

I should not have to listen so long as I don't say anything mean!

Why do I have to listen to other kids talking about things that I think are boring?

You may wonder why people say that you need to listen more to what your friends are saying. It may make more sense if you can think about how frustrated you would feel if someone told you what you were talking about was "boring." Your feelings would be hurt if they walked away while you were in the middle of telling them about a game you just made up or were showing them a new present.

Part of being a friend is showing interest in what your friend is saying and doing, even if it is not your idea or favorite activity.

It might help if I:

- show interest in what my friend is telling me about and then ask if I can tell them about something that I think is cool

- see if I can remember three things about what my friend told me and tell them to my parents later in the day

- ask my friend if I can play with the toy that they just described.

Do you have any ideas of what might help you become more interested in things that other people like a lot?

Ready to listen.

3

Rules that may be Frustrating about School

It's boring to listen to the same thing over and over again.

Why do I have to listen to the teacher talking about something that I already know?

You might feel frustrated when a teacher asks you to listen to them talk about something that you think you already know. The reason that teachers want everyone to listen to what they are saying is so they can make sure that everyone is learning the same thing. Different teachers may teach different ways to solve the same math problem or write a story. If you listen carefully, you may learn something new each time you read the same book or hear the same story. It may help you to remember that scientists often spend a long time studying the same thing; they are always looking for new things that they did not see the first time they studied the material.

It can be fun to learn new things about the same topic.

When my teacher is talking about something familiar to me, I could:

- see if I can remember what happens to a specific character in the story

- remember that learning a new way to do something does not mean my way was wrong

- see if my teacher explains a topic the same way that I remember it; if I learned something else about the same subject, then I can share that with my teacher at the end of the day.

Do you have any ideas that might help you enjoy listening to a story that you have already heard before, or learning about a subject that you know something about?

Ready to learn something new.

I don't understand why I have to use things if I don't like the way they feel!

Why do I have to do things that get my hands dirty?

It would be nice if you did not have to touch things that feel funny on your hands. Sometimes, if you let yourself try a few times, you might find out that you enjoy it. You might like building in the sand, pounding clay, or painting once you get used to how the different things feel on your hands.

You may want to try touching one new thing at a time until you feel comfortable using it. Remember, at the end of your play or art time you always will be able to clean your hands.

I could:

- rub my hands together hard before the activity; this may help it not feel so funny

- get some special cleaning gel for school and use it to wash my hands between activities; this way I will not need to go to the bathroom to clean off my hands

- explore playing with these different materials at home

- keep a chart of all of the new things that I have played with and touched

- set up a reward chart with my parents for trying new materials.

Do you have any ideas that might help you explore and play with materials that feel funny on your hands?

Ready to get my hands dirty.

I like to give friends a big hug and a pat on the back!

Why do I have to say "Hello" with words?

It may not seem fair that you get in trouble for giving your friend a big hug or surprise greeting from behind. You probably were not trying to hurt your friend, but most people do not like other people touching their bodies. It will help to remember that nobody likes to be pushed, squeezed, or hit very hard. Most people also do not like to have other people bump into them, surprise them, cover their eyes or pull their arms from behind; this can scare them and make them feel angry. Can you remember how you felt when someone bumped into you at school?

It is always best to make sure that your friend is not in the middle of doing something, and then say "Hello" while you are facing them.

It is nice to have friends that respect each other's bodies.

I could:

- ask my friend if it is OK to give them a big hug or sit close to them before I do it

- find objects rather than people that I can push, pull, or bump into – like a trampoline, tetherball, wagon, class-room wall, or big bean bag pillow!

Do you have any ideas that might help keep you from hugging a friend too hard or bumping into them by surprise?

Ready to greet my friends.

I should be able to tell the class about any interesting things I know!

Why do I have to answer only the last question the teacher asked?

You might feel frustrated when your teacher only wants to hear your answer to the question they just asked. You may have raised your hand before you heard the last question or want to tell the class about something that is interesting to you. The reason that teachers only want to hear an answer to the question they just asked is that they have several different things they want to talk about during a class. When children talk about things that are not related to the last question, then their comments can be confusing to both the teacher and the rest of the class.

If there is something else you want to tell the teacher you can tell them at the end of the class.

It's fun to learn new things in class.

It might help if I:

- tell myself to put all of the information I wanted to talk about in a pretend file and share it with the teacher at the end of the class

- pretend to be a detective, paying close attention to what the teacher asks, and raise my hand only when I know the answer to the question they just asked

- remind myself that it is OK not to know the answer to every question.

Do you have any other ideas about what may help you respond to just the last question that the teacher asked the class?

Ready to answer the question.

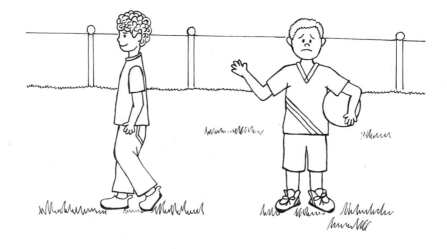

I don't know why I have to explain everything!

Why do I have to tell my friends that I am no longer playing the game when they can see for themselves?

Sometimes it may not seem fair when you get in trouble for leaving a game that you no longer want to play, especially if you decide to leave the game rather than get into an argument. At other times, you may not have told your friends what you were doing because you thought they could tell. It is important to remember that most of the time other people cannot tell what you are thinking if you do not tell them with words. For example, if you suddenly decide to stop playing a game of tag, then your friends may think that you are still hiding and spend a lot of time looking for you.

It is important to let your friends know if you are going to leave a game.

It's fun to play different games with friends.

It may help if I:

- play a game of charades with my parents and friends and see if they can tell what I am doing, and if I can tell what they are doing without using words

- call a friend by their name, make sure that they are looking at me and then tell them, "I'm not playing any more."

- ask the other kids, "Do you want to play another game?"

Do you have any other ideas about what might help you tell a friend when you want to stop playing a game?

Ready to explain what I am doing.

I don't like having to ask my teacher for permission to do everything!

Why do I have to ask my teacher if it is OK to leave the room?

There might be times when you need to leave the room. When you leave the room to go to the bathroom, you may need to ask your teacher if it is OK. You might think that it is obvious where you are going, but your teacher would be very worried if they did not know where you were.

When you get frustrated, you may think that it is better for you to go outside to cool down, but your teacher and principal would be very worried and upset if you went outside without getting their permission, because they are responsible for your safety at school. Most classrooms have times when you can and cannot leave your class.

Depending on your class rules, you might always need to ask an adult if it is OK for you to go to the bathroom or go to a "cool down" area.

It is nice to know that the adults at school want to keep you safe.

It might help if I:

⇨ ask the teacher the best ways to tell them when I need to leave the room, either to go to the bathroom, calm down, or get some exercise

⇨ ask the teacher if I can use a card for those times when it's very hard for me to talk

⇨ choose a "safe place" with my teacher where I can go when I need some quiet time to cool down if I get upset.

Do you have any other ideas about what might help you remember to let people know when you want to leave a room or an activity?

Ready to communicate with the teacher.

I work best when I am standing up or lying down!

Why do I have to sit at my desk at school when I am doing my work?

This rule may not make any sense to you if you feel more comfortable working while you are standing up or lying down on the floor. You may feel like you do your best work when you are the most comfortable. The reason that most teachers want you to work at your desk is so you do not disrupt the people sitting next to you. If you work standing up the person sitting behind you will not be able to see the teacher or the board.

If you work best standing up or lying down, you may be able to create a special working space in the back or on the side of the classroom where you can go to do your work, without disrupting the other children.

It is important to find a way to work in the classroom that is good for you and for your classmates.

It might help if I:

- talk to my teacher or an occupational therapist about ways to make working at a desk more comfortable

- explore if it helps to take an exercise break in between my work

- figure out if I don't like sitting at my desk only with certain activities or at certain times of the day.

Do you have any other ideas about how you may make working in your classroom more comfortable?

Ready to sit down to work.

My humming doesn't bother me at all!

Why do I have to be quiet when I am working?

It can be frustrating when you get in trouble for making different sounds while you are working, if they do not bother you. Some people who are sensitive to sounds are bothered by the sounds that other people make. It may be hard for you to tell when your voice is OK or if it is bothering someone. Some people make sounds because they like the way that it feels in their mouth. It is OK to make sounds while you are working in a private area, like your bedroom, den, or a private study room.

It's nice when people are considerate of other people.

If other people hear me make sounds while I work, I could:

- make a tape or video recording of myself doing home-work at home and/or at school so that I can listen to the sounds that I make when I am working

- try seeing if it helps to chew on something resistive (like baby carrots) or suck on something hard (like hard candy or drinking through a sports water bottle)

- make a sign to put on my desk to remind me not to make sounds while I am working

- try listening to special music using headphones so I do not have to make the noises myself

- ask my occupational therapist for some ideas of things that I could try at home or at school.

Do you have any other ideas of what might help you remember not to make sounds while you are doing your work at school?

Ready to work quietly.

If they were watching then they would know!

Why do I have to explain to an adult why I got into a fight?

It may seem impossible that the playground teacher did not see everything that happened when you got into an argument with another student. It seems that way because you were the one having the disagreement. Afterward, you may have been able to tell the teacher what the other child did to you, but you may not be able to remember how the argument started, or what happened before you began to fight.

It is impossible for teachers to see and hear everything that occurs on the playground. That is why the playground teacher, your teacher, and the principal may ask everyone to explain what they think happened. It is important to remember that the person you were arguing with will probably have seen things differently than you.

Most of the time the adults cannot be sure who was right and who was wrong, but instead they punish both sides for getting into a fight.

It's always better to find somebody to talk to rather than getting into a fight.

If someone is bothering me, I could:

- ✐ find another activity to do rather than argue with the person bothering me

- ✐ remember that the person who is bothering me may be trying to upset me and get me in trouble

- ✐ if I am upset, ask the teacher on duty for help.

Do you have any ideas of what might help you prevent getting into an argument on the playground?

Ready to sort things out.

I am too tired to work at home after being in school all day!

Why do I have to do homework after I have been working in school all day?

It may not seem fair that teachers expect you to do more school-work after school, at home. You may feel like there is no time left in your day to do what you like to do. The reason that most teachers give homework is that there is not enough time during the school day to finish all of the work you need to do.

If you are having a very difficult time getting your homework done, then you and your parents can talk with your teacher and see if there is a way to make doing homework less frustrating for you. You may spread your work out during the week so that you do not have so much to do every night, or see if you can reduce how much you need to do.

Doing homework does not mean that you cannot have any fun at home; it just means that you have to find a better way to get it done so that it does not take over all of your time.

It might help if I:

- choose a special time in the afternoon or evening and a space to do my homework

- see if I move my body before sitting, which may help me tolerate sitting again

- keep a record of how much time I spend doing work and how much time I spend playing

- have a meeting with my teacher and parents so that we can find a better way for me to get my work done.

Do you have any ideas about how to make homework work better for you?

Ready to go and have fun.

Appendix 1

What Frustrates Me, and What Might Help

As you grow older, you may find that some of the rules that did not make sense to you when you were younger make more sense to you now. You may also find new rules that do not seem fair. I hope that this book has helped you understand some of the rules that frustrate you, and given you some ideas for how you might be able to work with these rules rather than against them.

Write down below any rules that may frustrate you and your ideas of what you could do to make them easier for you to follow.

✏ I do not understand why:

. . . .

. . . .

. . . .

✏ It makes me feel:

. . . .

. . . .

. . . .

✏ The reasons why I need to:

. . . .

. . . .

. . . .

✏ Some things that I could do are:

. . . .

. . . .

. . . .

✏ I do not understand why:

. . . .

. . . .

. . . .

✏ It makes me feel:

. . . .

. . . .

. . . .

✏ The reasons why I need to:

. . . .

. . . .

. . . .

✏ Some things that I could do are:

. . . .

. . . .

. . . .

✏️ I do not understand why:

. . . .

. . . .

. . . .

✏️ It makes me feel:

. . . .

. . . .

. . . .

✏️ The reasons why I need to:

. . . .

. . . .

. . . .

✏️ Some things that I could do are:

. . . .

. . . .

. . . .

✏ I do not understand why:

. . . .

. . . .

. . . .

✏ It makes me feel:

. . . .

. . . .

. . . .

✏ The reasons why I need to:

. . . .

. . . .

. . . .

✏ Some things that I could do are:

. . . .

. . . .

. . . .

Appendix 2

My Goal Chart

Some possible goals:

- ✏ sharing

- ✏ using my words

- ✏ being a good friend

- ✏ getting ready on time

- ✏ staying calm

- ✏ making sure me and my friends are looking at each other before talking.

Goal: . . . .

Date	Before school	After school	Dinner	Before bed	After bed	Notes
Monday						
Tuesday						
Wednesday						
Thursday						
Friday						

Date	7 am to 10 am	10 am to 1 pm	1 pm to 4 pm	4 pm to 7 pm	7 pm to 10 pm	Notes
Saturday						
Sunday						